Inside a Factory

Table of Contents

by Allie Benton

Getting Started

A toy **store** can be a fun place to go. At a toy store, you can buy a baseball bat, a box of crayons, a bike, or even a video game.

Did you ever think about where your toys came from? Your toys were made in a **factory**. Let's take a peek inside.

What Is a Factory?

A factory is a place where things are made. Some things are made from **raw materials** such as plastic, cloth, or grapes.

The raw materials come into the factory. Then they are made into things people can buy.

Plastic may be made into toy cars. Grapes may be made into jam. Cloth may be made into jeans. Later, people can buy these things in stores.

Workers and Machines

Machines do many of the jobs in a factory. A machine can put wheels on bikes or put labels on bottles.

Factories need people, too. Some people run the machines. Others may fix the machines, pack boxes, load trucks, or clean up.

This **worker** drives a forklift. He takes boxes from place to place.

This worker helps out in the office of the factory. She pays the bills. She also keeps track of what things stores have ordered.

A Visit to a Crayon Factory

Let's look inside one special factory. This factory makes crayons.

A crayon is made of wax and colored powder. These are the raw materials used to make crayons.

First, the wax is melted. Then it is placed into large metal pots called *vats*. Now it's time to add colored powder to the wax. The hot colored wax will be used to make crayons.

How a Crayon Is Made

Step 1

Step 2

Step 1: The hot wax is poured into molds. Each hole in the mold is the shape of a crayon.

Step 2: The crayons are taken out of the molds. A worker checks to make sure none of the crayon tips are broken.

Step 3   **Step 4**

Step 3: A color label is glued onto each crayon. The crayons are ready to be packed in boxes.

Step 4: A machine fills the boxes with different colored crayons.

The boxes of crayons are packed into big crates. These crates are sent to stores all over the world. Children in places as far away as Japan or Mexico may use the crayons made in this factory.

Fun Facts

- Crayons have been made for more than 100 years. In 1903, a box of crayons cost five cents.

- Today, one factory can make more than 12 million crayons a day!

- Most kids will use 730 crayons by the time they are 10 years old.

- Crayons come in more than 100 different colors.

Index